We Interrupt
these Wars

Allegra Jordan

*Poems of grace in the face of the unbearable and
irreversible*

*To Mr & Mrs
Russ
Pool*

*With thanks
for all you do*

for so many

[signature]

2021

Allegra Jordan/Gold Gable Press
Blundering Heights
105 Pebble Springs Road, Chapel Hill NC 27514
www.allegrajordan.com

Cover photo: Ted walking the Irish Coast by Allegra Jordan, 2019.

Book Layout © 2017 BookDesignTemplates.com

We Interrupt These Wars/ Allegra Jordan. 1st ed.

Dedication

To all my fellow classmates in
life's crash course
on "Letting Go."

Contents

We Interrupt These Wars

At Cluny

Tell me a tale of the earth made new
By complicated men who built strong walls
To cloister gardens and heal souls and who
Brought light to our world after Rome's fall.
In Burgundy's gardens leaders arose
Who taught the world to flourish, to learn, sing
And sculpt a vision of our tomorrows.
Even in ruins, I see its wellspring.
This old tale of new life is worth telling,
For I am the daughter of a soldier
And war's long reach invaded my dwelling.
I became a midwife to help shoulder
Love's rebirth. Cluny, lend us your story
So we too may rest in peace and rise in glory.

Western Europe emerged from the Dark Ages in large part due to the Cluny monastery system in Burgundy, France, which cultivated wholesome communities, education, health and the arts.

Black Turtles

And drive past the stone church to the water
In March or April when the river rushes
Around the rocks where black turtles sun.
They hear with their bones, and politely so.
As you read the Easter story, listen
To what the waters in your heart mutter
About the long years of loneliness
Where you withdrew under cold river ice.
Check your compass cracked when liars climbing
Over your betrayal-benumbed back pushed off.
You know exactly how long it has been
Since it felt wise to breathe.
Sapphire-blue butterflies dance around you.
The pollen of primavera stings
Your eyes. Spring is a possibility
If the harrowing of Hades is past.
Then listen with your warming bones beyond
The sound of sour chokecherries budding
And the poisoned sepals of the staggerbush.
As unbidden tears arise, a space appears.
Will your bones hear the wild God
Who offers you communion?

Deep Beauty in the Broken Earth

To see a flower in the Spring, we must
Believe that there is beauty to be had
In gardens we never will control. "Trust
And hope that dirt becomes a launching pad
For raising beauty in this violent earth?"
The cynics scoff but have no solutions,
Because they do not know what beauty's worth.
Despair's enchanting, but contributions
To healing the heart's hidden wounds require
A deeper balm than despair can give us.
Consider that beauty can re-inspire
The dry bones of life with a delicious
Wonder. Renew your love affair with life
By planting beauty in the midst of strife.

Eudaimonia (Flourishing)

It means to flourish. The ancient unread
Forgotten texts say this is our purpose.
The word echoes across time bankrupted
By the lies our eyes show us. The circus
And breads and gleaming bits sold for pleasure
Will bring no relief to an aching heart
Until one rests and roots into treasure
That was ours by right of birth. "That's a start,"
You may say. "But life is also brutal
And pain we did not know we could bear
Will blast away easy answers. It's futile
To think humans can flourish when despair
Finds us." But, I ask, "What's our duty
In the face of both evil and beauty?"

4

Who Will I Become Today?

Who will I become today? For I have
Freedom to explore the vast reach of space
Or time or mind or heart and even grave.
In this moment, with this breath, I can chase
The rambling rills of Irish hills, design
A flower park or play guitar with Bach.
To tune my soul to seek this space of mind
And spirit–such a lovely spot–I dock
And dip my feet in springs of love needed
For humans to flourish. Empathy,
Genuine respect, warmth, caring proceeded
Any hope of finding this blessedly
Beautiful place. Such conditions revive
And keep my imagination alive.

To Coleridge

The morning sun bursts through the maple's leaves
Illuminating spiders' silver webs.
The hosta and rose I can now perceive
Are woven together. As the dawn ebbs
The glittering unifying cords fade
From perception. I smile. Perception!
Perception is Imagination's bondmaid.
Is She a projection–a deception?
Or the echoes of a creative light
That require a lifetime for my eyes
To reckon with, to befriend, to delight?
I catch glimpses. My perception belies
The truth. And yet, light still calls to light
From Eden's dawn to my dimmed inner sight.

Seasons of Suffering

Suffering–"I'm not OK"–has seasons.
From time to time we're summoned to confront
A new lack of wholeness that comes for reasons
We may or might not deserve. The affront
Will confront the "me I was:" Grow or die.
And I must meet the new, unfinished "me"
That I'm now. Truths that once would fortify
My soul have vanished. I'm an amputee
In agony, alone and not OK.
Yet only now can reintegration
Be possible. And as I ricochet
Between loss and hope, a new creation
Is born. It's hard. As I walk these days of wrath
May love and grace and angels guide my path.

Getting Cheddared

Some very fine cheese is made by squeezing
Constituent components so hard
That the curds mash together, easing
The way to bandage them up, discard
Residual whey – feed it to the pigs!–
Age it and voilà: an excellent cheese.
But not all cheese is made that way. Cheese gigs
Come with all sorts of different ways to tease
Out milk's poetry. Cheddaring is just
One approach to making cheese. But maybe
One day you are done with being smashed. Trust
Your gut as much as you trust rennet to be
A catalyst to new life that's better
Than another round of getting cheddared.

Nursing A Courage Hangover

When we live a courageous life, some days
Will be better than others. Know your goals.
You get to be you, grow and reappraise
The arc of your life. You may change your role
And frighten your friends. They change too you'll find.
Some promising friendships just don't flourish.
Some hurt. This happens to us all. Unwind
Friendships that did, but no longer, nourish.
And notice where you're vulnerable to guilt
And over-functioning. Ask "Why am I
Abandoning my dreams?" You are not built
To deny your life. Be your best ally.
This takes courage. It may hurt for a while.
But where your heart weeps, your soul may smile.

*The Sufi poet Rumi wrote, "When the heart weeps for what it
has lost, the soul laughs for what it has found."*

I See the Assassins Have Failed

"Good morning. I see the assassins have failed:"
Now that's a funny quote to put on mugs.
But yes. Yes they failed. They may have impaled
My wallet. Where I sought love, they sent thugs.
But my deepest soul was not seized.
I ran and hid and ducked and I don't know why
My soul survived and was not diseased
By death. Why not give up and say good-bye
To life's crash-course in letting go? But I
Am here. Somehow the "Yes" inside of me
Never became a final "No." Why–
I cannot say. It's a real mystery.
But I'm thankful that today I've a "Yes"
To continue this life's work-in-progress.

Writing the Apology I'll Never Get

I wrote letters of remorse I'll not get
From those who should have written me but won't.
My first draft was raw and wrong as I let
My head hold the pen. Not my heart. Don't
Ever stop once you begin because
The thing your soul needs to hear may hide
Behind what you think your soul felt when claws
Got too close and hurt you. Take your own side
And listen: What does your soul long to hear?
And if you can't get what you want, what need
Asks for kind attention? Is there a tear
You need to witness? And if so, sweet
Relief may be found a ghosted letter.
Make it full-throated! You may feel better.

A Psalm of Lament

Quickly inhale.
My eyes wide open.
Where am I?
What is wounded? broken? what now?
A gash, a tear, a shattered hip.
Bandages? Would they even work?
Quick! Antiseptic.
Move? You must be joking.
Can't you see I'm blown apart?
You are serious! I can't stay here?
What do you mean "get up"?
Where is my health? My family?
Why? How? It's awful
To be broken in a bombing.
Let me sit and cry.
The alarm sounds. It's not safe here.
Stay and I'll dissolve into the stained soil.
JESUS H CHRIST
Don't let this take too long.
Touch my hip
Let me limp beside the many women
Whose story I now share.
I know I should ask you to
Put love where there was nitrate.
Put grace where there was a fuse.
But all I want is for you to
Calm the ringing in my ears.
Until I can sleep again.
When will it be
That I find my rest in Thee?

Croak

I wish God did not respect my freedom
So much. God would keep me from grasping for
The delicious temptation of "I'm right."
I feel like such a toad, blinkered in mud,
When I bring debate to a dogma fight.

The Wind & the Waterfall

In wild, woolly Wales
I saw the wind blow
A waterfall back up its hill.
The rain was hard and
Kicked the stream down the steep hill
To where it could not but fall down that rocky canyon.
But that swollen stream met its match at
A slated edge not fifteen feet from the roadside
Where the wind refused to cooperate with gravity.
And the water, with nowhere to turn
Did a back flip.
And flew part into the wind to go to new places
And part back into the stream to try again.
I've been that waterfall.
And by right and reason I was going down
Pulled by gravity,
Kicked by some,
Pushed by my own failings,
Falling rapidly in my despair.
The breath that refused to let me fall
Caught me by surprise.
YOU ARE NOT DONE YET.
It flung me back with confidence
And refused my surrender to gravity.
I became mist.
I became a different stream.
And the shocked onlookers
One of whom was me
Had a new story to tell.

What Makes Creatures Curious?

Do you wonder why you wonder? What is
Behind that spark that sets chemicals
Adrift in your bean? What analysis
Did you imbibe from a polemical,
Academical biology book
About that which makes creatures curious?
Don't be blinkered by the gobbledygook
Of correlates. You are a glorious
Fantastic creature unexplainable
By single synaptic gospels science
Illuminates. What is attainable:
To search for your spirit in defiance
Of mechanical explanations. Find
The soul behind the synapse. Treat it kind.

Thin Spaces

("/Thin spaces/ are locales where the distance
between heaven and earth collapses and we're able to
catch glimpses of the divine, or the transcendent." –
Eric Weiner, "Where Heaven & Earth Come Closer,"
New York Times, May 12, 2012)

Into the raucous rumpus of a wedding
I came with a cold but left with a
Warm sense I'd walked into thin spaces
I'd feared to go because I was not ready.
Connecting without harm
To the powerful energy of love
Is tricky business.
There cannot be too much of me, nor too little trust.
Just the right amount, and maybe the ground opens
Our entangled particles pull us
In a great communal leap
Across the chasm of old, familiar pain
To a new we.
If we do this right we're lighter & freer.
We do this wrong we come out bitter, dirty, tired.
It's a tricky business.
Thin spaces surprise you
Like the Spanish Inquisition.
Ready to pounce and strip you
Until at your core you know
Who you are.
What you want to become.
Thin spaces don't appear on a time-stamped agenda.
They don't like being ordered around.
They are not boasting or vain.
Praise a thin space and it disappears for decades.
They are not idols, but portals.

Pay attention to the right things:
Nuances, gestures, hesitations, the excuse.
Why is she here? That's a good start.
What does she seek? Even better.
What is going on?
God-given mishaps are thin-space language
That transform a moldy, dusty surface with a
Truth no language would approach
and you'd never find IF
-the lunch started on time or
-the key was in the right pocket, and
-the trash didn't stink in the ante-chamber
forcing people together inside to what could be
a tomb or a passage to a new world.
A soft knock outside a locked door.
Must be careful as she enters.
In that moment I trust the light
That shines on her face will show
Kindness in her eyes even if it's just
The reflection of the wish in mine.
Come in.
Sit.
Drink.
Let me tell you a funny story
Where I failed.
And in our laughter,
We fall gently into that thin space
To a new world
Where I must be as aware of who I am
As I was in the last.
There are no shortcuts.
Pay attention.
That's the rule of thin space law.
See what's before you not what you wish to see.
Look too much for the girl in the dress and
You'll miss the knock on the door.
Long for the knock and miss the person at your side.
A shorter cab ride for two and
You miss the bridge for three

To a new future from a dead past.
Take pictures too fast and miss the waiting around
Where the real miracle occurs
A brief confession.
Reconciliation –
a taste sweeter than all the wine of Cana.
Roll up a wedding into a watch and find
It's 1% I do –
A beautiful sigh for all to enjoy
But 99% is where the miracles are found.
We know they love each other, but do we?
Somewhere in all the waiting are
Thin spaces overstretched hearts can stumble through.
It's only waiting around if you're
Blind to
God-sightings
Grace-catchings and
Dappled light
From the other world restored,
Unbroken
Soft and
Kind.

El Morro

"Was it hell to build?" I ask.
"The lash, the ox, the muscles straining
To forge this invincible fortress?
Tell me your story El Morro.
I come from a land
Under a different sun and
Have not heard your name before."

I perch on the parapet of its giant wall
As an osprey and egret fly overhead.
A pelican plunges into the sea
And a mottled cat stalks a lizard.

El Morro answers:

"Climb closer and see.
The walls are wide.
You will not fall.
Take off your shoes and
Let your feet free.

I am El Morro. An old man
Who loves to play.

In my youth I controlled blood-red seas
Through whips, shackles, and tumbrel rides.
But five hundred years later
The sea changed and I was released
From combat to rest.

Now the sea is brilliant teal
Edged with a white confetti
Tossed by the waves as they

Crash onto the rocks.
That crash is our only violence now.

I've lost my white walls.
Ferns grow in cracks
Where no ferns should grow.
And under the moonlight
The only sentries now are lovers.
They come two by two to kiss.
The heat of their embrace
Warms my walls every night.
Together we smile by the sea.

Oh young child,
Lend me your innocence
And I'll give you my strength.
You cannot stand in a place
I didn't touch first.
You will not catch trade winds
If I do not let you pass.
But with my blessing,
You'll face the sea dogs
With *fortes* and fresh water.
My eyes will watch you, and
My breath will fill your sail,
As you bob in your boat,
Beyond the curve of the earth.

Child

Climb closer and see what
Lovers carved on me
One night by moon:
'Te Adoro. I love you fer evah.'

Cardiff Bay

The stiff gray winds of Cardiff Bay
Push along white swans
Yellow & green grass dance in the wetlands.
The sun is up.
All is in motion now.
There is no solid ground once you leave shore.
To venture forth
You must
Feel the waves, and
Divine the path.
It's not ballet
But a tango
Where the next step is made best by
Paying attention
To what's
Before you,
In you,
Around you,
&
The music your soul is tuned to hear.

Walking Hadrian's Wall

Maps

This one takes me from Hexham to Gilsland
Along Hadrian's Wall.
And what did I think I'd find?
I stretch back in my mind a decade ago when the idea came
During a divorce in the making. My broken heart
Called to my brother (in a rough patch himself).
"One day we'll get through this mess
And we'll want to plan something as outlandishly good
As this time has been terribly bad.
May I suggest Hadrian's Wall
For my love of the windy North
And yours for Roman eagles?"
Over the years the dust settled and the kids grew
And money was never in supply.
Then one day an letter came to us
From mother, a frugal pensioner.
"Hadrian's Wall," was all it said, check enclosed.
I never had faith I'd be here.
I never knew I'd have the time or funds.
I never knew when we'd leave, but here we are.
I bought this map of the Wall to plot our path.
But to map the heart, I'll draw a poem.
Time for new stories.

Rucksacks

I see men and women impossibly young
Pass us en masse,
Their hair up or cut off,
Their rucksacks desert camo.
They run, doubletime, along the cliffs
Along the Emperor's wall.
I suppose it's been that way
Since Jesus' day:
Warriors, forever young,
Running the Emperor's wall.
They run the Emperor's wall.

Vallum

That ditch is a trap
Set for those coming and going
Who want life beyond the wall.
It may feel like death to be in that ditch
But–let me break this to you gently–
You're still alive.
Gather your wits and get to work.
So push on or bargain; retreat, fly, dance, cuss
Beg, protest, sing for your supper or tell a funny story
But standing still is not an option.
Get off your knees. Get up.
And get on with the business of life.

Coventina

"The muddy patch you'll want to avoid,"
The ruddy-faced tourist points to a ditch.
But we're all tourists here.
I pop on my pack and begin to walk.
Unstable rocks shift in the mud;
As I wait my turn to cross the mire
I spy a yolk-yellow wildflower
Splattered by drops of red.
I've never seen this before.
And I look beyond it in the ditch
And it's not just one
On a green stalk so proud but
A whole vallum of yellow and red
Easy to miss if you're just looking for mud.
Only later I find this unmarked spring
With its Blood-drop Emlets
Was once sacred to Coventina
A British goddess who was a river of kindness.
I see she still waters beauty
For those who stop and look.

Stone Blindness

The massive, dominating stone wall
Demands you knuckle under.
Built in six months
You must admit you can't do that
No matter how strong and determined you are.
Yet it's not the wall I see today
But the hills of Northumbria
Wild violets, yellow buttercup, white daisies
And the sheep's bleat and the cows eat grass
And the rams converse while the young gambol
And I realize I have stone blindness,
What the mason says is the inability to see rocks
For what they are anymore.
In fact, I've not seen the rocks since Hexham
Though I've walked beside them for miles.

An Englishman at Walltown Crags

Further in the journey
We're all less chatty now.
Feet sore, supplies low
The novelty of the pilgrimage wore off a few hills back.
The Englishman from yesterday
Who passed by our picnic with a cheerful greeting
Is standing and looking down at his felt hat.
"Still headed to Carlisle?" I ask. "Quite a walk from here."
He's looks like Knightley
But sighs like Dumbledore:
"You get these great ideas," he says,
"And now my hat is broken
And I'm wondering about bus schedules."
It dawns on me that he too may be a poet.

Housesteads

Eight miles up and down
To reach Housesteads
A Roman fort replete with history
So rich it's called
To soldiers and pilgrims and raiders
For thousands of years.
And when I get there
–Breathless with delight–
I head past the gate
To the car park's porta-potty
And then to the till of the English Trust
Where I buy a ticket to the site.
And finding the Roman prefect's home abandoned
I make a bed on its grass,
Unsullied by sheep
And take a delicious nap
While my brother, a Latin teacher,
Bounds, a happy kid, around ruins.

The Spinner

A wiry young man bends before a pile of rocks
Under a blue sky in the stone fields of Vindolanda
Picking up bits of rock
Turning them over
Again and again
Under a rushing wind and warm sun so kind.
The day is so perfect you think it's a fake.
In the distance, a gaggle of archeologists cheer
Their finding a cheese sieve and another shoe.
The master stone mason
Alone in the field,
Exposed with his windstone,
Spins and spins
And suddenly puts it down
His smile an outward sign
Of inward cheer
For the perfect stone fit.

An Archeologist Takes His Breakfast

The remains of his feast
Beyond the eggs and b.
Are strewn across the farmhouse table.
The archeologist we met that morning
Manspread paper and books by the burned toast.
Before our party arrived.
Never having breakfasted with such a bird
I sat beside him to see what I could learn.
He'd come to examine Birdoswold
For his county's newsletter–
And before my first cup was drained
He'd shared the secrets of his entire industry,
The history of the wall and what one does
With a plate if at an altar.
And so I learned that breakfast
With British diggers
Can be a two-handed affair.
With one discover the past
And with the other you take a trowel-full of words and jam
To create a great gulf between human hearts
So that the other will never be seen.
I left the table hungry having only eaten
A full English breakfast.

Northumbrian Heights

I remember trembling trekking cliff-side
Up Arthur's Seat in Scotland.
I didn't make it.
Three years later I was back and ready to attack
But was defeated again by fear. Shamed,
I walked around the back and learned
I could get to the top that way too.
Curious.
And like a warming sun, I slowly learned
To enjoy cliff-side beauty.
There was no tremble in my stomach
Or weakness in my gait.
Or heart pumping, palms sweating
And mouth running about how heights are not for me.
I healed somewhere back there.
Just where, I can't say.
Few know the moment they are healed.
But suddenly you look out and there's no fear between you
And the great wide world.
And you bless the path that raised you up.

Peace Ascending

The Empire's Wall lies in ruin,
Moss grown and mottled
In lush green and golden fields.
After Empire came Arthur, and Æthelflæd
Viking and Norman and a thousand years
Of generals and kings and raids and battles.
Who was it that kept the faith
That peace would one day
Descend into the vallum,
And plunder walls, hearts and souls
So thoroughly that
Now, at rosy dawn we find
This grizzled veteran of a wall
Overrun
By children's laughter and pilgrims' sighs
All in love with sights and sounds of peace.

Summer Solstice
on the
Wild Atlantic Way

Shedding

I stop talking.
The words go first
As I turn inward.
I'm grateful for this time of shedding.
I need a rested heart.
Appearing dormant, I'm anything but.
My memory flies to cool water
And a warm sun where I can
Let go of locked jaw
And send my tired old fears
Into a Great Dismal Swamp.
No, not the one in Carolina
The one in me I need to drain.
If I shed today and tomorrow
And tomorrow and tomorrow–
Such a petty, creeping pace–
I've faith I'll hunger for life again.
Perhaps a month or two from now
A luscious bit will cross my path.
I'll catch it and it will be delicious.
Today it would taste like cardboard.

Seeing

I see daisies near Ireland's Western shore
Perhaps one for each starved soul
From the Great Famine which was not so great
For those who starved.
And I ask why miracles should abound
For raspberries, thistle and buttercup?
And how can the soil and water nurture
Magellan's Fuchsia and fields of clover
But not the land's children?
And I realize I'm asking God
But not my fellow man who holds the keys
To solve such riddles.

Shoo Fly!

Shoo fly! I'm meditating.
I flew to Ireland to sit and
Rejuvenate and
My irritation with you is
More fun to ponder than the bird,
The sheep, the mountain, the lake and–
LORD JESUS
I am doing it again.
Ommmmmm.
Ommmmmm.
If it weren't for that stupid fly
I'd be Gandhi.

Pilgrimage

1. Faith

When two country cars meet
Along a single lane
The council assumes they'll figure it out.
It's so much cheaper
Than building a second lane
And assuming folks can't agree to agree
When it's their own lives at stake.

2. A Murder of Crows

Crows, rooks and blackbirds
Not yet baked in a pie
In city and country look
Scraggly, plucked and scraped.
A rough crowd, I hear.
I even hear the gangs near Bantry
Still teach *The Raven*
In their murders.

3. Rammed

The black ram gamboled towards us
Its rounded horns pointed down to fight.
My husband makes three quick bleats.
The ram looks away.
It wants no part of crazy.

4. Irish Cows

Oh to be an Irish cow!
To amble by the ocean
To roll in clover –
Not a metaphor, but the source of many–
To dive into wild angelica and pink yarrow face first
And find it three inches deeper than you thought.
You've found the softest mattress
In a world of hurt. It is udder delight.
"Forgive me," the cow says, closing its eyes
And, head against the earth, falls to sleep.
I envy its muscular bulk.
Its chest rises *andante*
To crashing waves below the cliff,
Its sighs as an alto who finally finished
The Ring Cycle and can now go to bed.
I wonder if its music that's the reason
Why Irish butter tastes so good.

Cliffs

In Ireland I learned again the two ways
To sit at the top of a cliff.

The first is to go face first up
Ocean-splashed blue slate walls.
Your hands strain and heart races
And your chest heaves
While Atlantic waves crash
Below and rooks bicker above.

The other way is to come from the back,
Traverse a plateau,
Across a flower-filled turf so soft
If you stumble you trip over beauty:
Royal Ferns, ochre lichens
And a thousand pink Ragged Robins.
How did God forget the thorns?
And if you fall, you plant your face
In a soft patch of lavender bluets
And smell a world fresh and new.

Reaching the cliff top you stretch out
Either like Prometheus offering his liver
Or a god's beloved, blessed
And protected at the wild ocean's side.

The Beach at Barley Cove

Go face first into the cold Atlantic
And bottoms up into the Irish sky;
The sharp current holds you down
While white waves crash above you.
Your feet (that you can't feel) get to work
And when you've done–
A few heroic strokes out and back–
You leave the water
More alive than you've been in years.
You marvel at the white-haired woman
Who lapped you in the cove,
Emerging from water strangely warm.
The colors, she says, are brighter.
So is her soul.
"Birgit's awesome," the lifeguard whispers.
"Forty minutes each day no matter the weather."
I'll be back tomorrow.

An Irish Jig

I'd heard about the Irish healing wells
But had not made time for one.
So one rainy morning just past the Solstice
I went behind the house
And stripped and stood ready to take
The beating Nature would give my body.
And though the wind was raw
The rain was not.
I went inside and was stunned
By the loveliness of it all.
Trotting my naked ass back out
I washed my face with wet ferns
And started to dance.
The wind blew up my lady parts:
Eye-poppingly fresh!
And that rainy, foggy morning
I went back out seven times
As Leper Naaman did in Two Kings.
The seventh time I climbed the crest
Of the highest hill by the Celtic Sea
And I paused to pray my thanks to fog and cloud
Who let no one see but the sea
My joy at dancing naked in the Irish rain.
.

The Choirs of County Cork

I wish they belled the cows and sheep
So choirs could play a duet with the wind
And form a symphony with the birds
And accompany a ballet of ferns waving along the verge.
I would listen with my eyes and ears and nose
On my way to take the cure
At O'Sullivan's Pub
And stop and know this–
This is the cure.

Where Cliffs & Cosmos Meet

I trace the map's thin roads
That got me here
And see them dwindle, dwindle
Into a path bounded with a bounce of daisies,
The sea in sight.
At the place where my cliff meets the cosmos
I jump into the hands of God
And fly with the crow
To western light bright and healing,
My heart bursts into love.
And falling gently to the sea,
I find myself reborn in
An ocean sparkling with light
Ready to begin anew.

.

About the Author

Named an "Architect of Change," by Maria Shriver, Allegra Jordan is the author of the World War I novel *The End of Innocence* (Sourcebooks, 2014) and two online collections of poetry at reconciliationpoetry.com and workpoems.com. Her articles, essays and cases have appeared in USA TODAY Harvard Business School Press, *Huffington Post*, Duke University's Faith and Leadership.com and other publications. She holds degrees from Harvard Business School and Samford University, and a certificate in leadership coaching from Georgetown University.

She works with a team near Ft. Bragg, the US' largest military installation by population, at a pilot reintegration park for active-duty service members in-between and post-deployment. The pilot park serves as the basis for a future national park system along the military highway that will support a generation of military children who have never known peace. For more information about Rick's Place, the reintegration park, please go to rhfnow.org.

For more information about Allegra please go to www.allegrajordan.com.